THE
OAHU COLLEGE
AT THE
SANDWICH ISLANDS.

BOSTON:
PRESS OF T. R. MARVIN, 42 CONGRESS STREET.
1856.

1817
ARTES
VERITAS
SCIENTIA
LIBRARY OF THE
UNIVERSITY OF MICHIGAN
E PLURIBUS UNUM
TUEBOR
SI QUÆRIS PENINSULAM AMŒNAM
CIRCUMSPICE

THE OAHU COLLEGE.

In the year 1841, a school was commenced, for the children of missionaries, at Punahou, near Honolulu, Sandwich Islands. Five years ago, it was opened to others besides the children of missionaries. The number of pupils has varied from thirty to sixty, and the whole number of pupils, up to September, 1854, was one hundred and twenty-two. In May, 1853, the Hawaiian Government incorporated twelve persons, all of them except one either then or formerly connected with the mission, as a corporate body by the name of "*The Trustees of the Punahou School and Oahu College.*" It is probable that the legal name of the institution will be shortened, and that it will be called simply the "*Oahu College.*"

The charter recognizes the design of the institution to be "the training of youth in the various branches of a Christian education, teaching them sound and useful knowledge." It further states, that, "as it is reasonable that the Christian education should be in conformity to the general views of the founders and patrons of the institution, no course of instruction shall be deemed lawful in said institution, which is not accordant with the principles of Protestant Evangelical Christianity, as held by that body of Protestant Christians in the United States of America, which originated the Christian mission to the Islands, and to whose labors and benevolent contri-

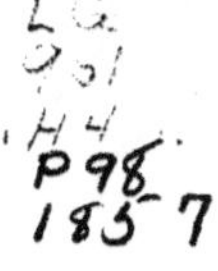

butions the people of these Islands are so greatly indebted." There is also an additional security for the institution in the following article, namely,—"Whenever a vacancy shall occur in said corporation, it shall be the duty of the Trustees to fill the same with all reasonable and convenient dispatch. And every new election shall be immediately made known to the Prudential Commitee of the American Board of Commissioners for Foreign Missions, and be subject to their approval or rejection, and this power of revision shall be continued to the American Board for twenty years from the date of this charter."

The Sandwich Islands Christianized.

The effort to christianize the Sandwich Islands, was begun in the year 1820, and has succeeded beyond any similar efforts recorded in history. In the year 1853, a little more than thirty years from the commencement of the mission, the Board was able to make proclamation in the Annual Report, that the people of the Sandwich Islands had become a Christian nation. The proofs then adduced of this fact were beyond all controversy; such as entitled the Hawaiian nation to the Christian name, if any people on earth might claim it; though without that intellectual development and social culture, which enter so deeply into the modern idea of civilization. But even in respect to these things a vast work had been accomplished.

It was evident to the Prudential Committee, as early as the year 1848, that the time had come for a change of some sort in the relations of the missionaries to the people of the Islands and to the Board. They saw that new and additional motives must be presented to induce the married missionaries to remain at the Islands, or the greater part of them might feel constrained to return to this country within a few years, to make provision for their children.

This was not owing simply, nor chiefly, to the number and age of their children, (for such a result was nowhere seen in the older missions elsewhere,) but to the novel and remarkable relations, at that time, of the mission to the people of the Sandwich Islands.

The problem, as then presented, was, how to give scope to the parental feelings in missionaries, without increasing burdens and expenses that could not be borne; though it soon appeared that there was really a higher problem to to be solved, and one that was novel in missions, namely, how to bring the mission itself, as such, to a termination, dissolving its relations to the Board, and merging its members in the newly created Christian community. The first problem stated came first in the order of time, and it involved the solution of the other. It was, how to convert the Islands into the home of the missionaries, (which the peculiar relation of the Islands to the commercial world then rendered possible,) and the missionaries into citizens and pastors. This was effected, so far as the action of the Prudential Committee was concerned, by a series of resolutions made public in the Report of the Board for the year 1849. The response of the missionaaries was in general favorable, though it required five years to complete the arrangement. The case was unprecedented; there was no experience; every step had to be considered in its principles, its equity, and its expediency. The transition was at length effected, and the mission was merged in the general Christian community of the Islands. The meeting of the mission in May, 1853, was its last meeting in its associated, corporate character as a mission,—responsible, as such, to the Board, controlling, as such, the operations of its members. The relations of the ministry and churches of the Sandwich Islands towards the Board and its patrons, and towards other foreign missions and the Christian church at large, then became those of an independent Christian community. The salaries of the native pastors, the cost of church buildings, and the greater part of the cost of schools, were to be met (as in fact they have been) by the natives. So was the support of Hawaiian missionaries, whether sent to Micronesia, or to the Marquesas Islands. It was only *in part,* however, that the natives could support their *foreign* pastors. The Board, in this new relation of things, would have to sustain to the new Christian community a relation like that, which the Home Missionary Society sustains to the Christian community in Oregon or California; and it might be necessary to continue this relation for some time.

Native College at Lahainaluna.

The first important step taken at the Islands after the mission had responded, in the year 1849, to the proposals of the Prudential Committee, was the transfer, by the Board, of the native Seminary or College at Lahainaluna to the Hawaiian Government. This is wholly for natives. The transfer was made on the condition, that the institution should continue to cultivate sound literature and science, and not allow to be taught religious doctrines contrary to those heretofore inculcated by the mission. In case of the non-fulfillment of the conditions, the whole property, with any additions and improvements made upon the premises, was to revert to the Board. The government have since sustained two clerical professors obtained from the company of missionaries, and the institution answers the purposes of a College for the native community. It is not adapted, however, nor can it be, to the wants of the foreign community.

Necessity for the College at Punahou.

The Oahu College is open to natives speaking the English language; but it is especially designed for pupils from that increasing and important portion of the Hawaiian community, which is of foreign origin. This of course includes those who have heretofore constituted the mission. These, with their families, must be regarded as in the highest degree essential to the religious welfare of the Islands. Their children, now at the Islands in a course of education, not including those too young for school, nor those in the colleges and schools of the United States, number one hundred and forty-five. To remove even a considerable portion of these for education to the United States, would be at great expense and inconvenience, and there is a growing conviction among the parents, that their children must be chiefly educated there. "They can there," says one of the most experienced of the parents, "be under parental guardianship and home influences; and this will help to retain both parents and children in the field. The education will be less perfect than in the United States, but it will fit them better, in some respects, to labor in the land of their birth, than an education in a foreign country. The parents will seek an education for their children elsewhere, if it be not provided for them at the Islands; but it is believed that most of them will retain their children there, if a college be there provided."

The number of foreign residents and their descendants is increasing at the Sandwich Islands. An intelligent glance at the future will show, that this enterprising community is destined to exert a very commanding influence in that increasingly important part of the world, and that the necessity of its being well educated cannot be overestimated. The foreign community now springing up at the Sandwich Islands will inevitably shape the character and destiny of the whole northern Pacific. The missionary part of this community has now the vantage ground as regards all good influences, and with the divine blessing is able to mould the literary and religious institutions of the Hawaiian nation. Religion, just now, has a strong hold on those Islands. The present is, therefore, a favorable time to institute a College, and put it into a working condition.

The necessity for an institution, such as it is proposed to make of the *Oahu College*, is one of the most obvious and interesting facts now presented to our view in that part of the world.

1. The College is essential to the development and continued existence of the Hawaiian nation. It is so because the missionary portion is really the *palladium* of the nation, and because a College is essential to that part of the community. The religious foreign community cannot otherwise long continue to perform its functions. It must have the means of liberally educating its children on the ground. Without a College, its moral, social and civil influence will tend constantly to decay. This most precious Christian influence, now rooted on the Islands, now no longer exotic, needs only the proper culture to perpetuate itself. The cheapest thing we can do for the Islands and for that part of the world, is to furnish this culture. It is better to educate our ministry there, than to send it thither from these remote shores. Indeed we are shut up to this, as our main policy. The providential indications are perfectly clear. Through the grace of God and the gospel of his Son, all the means, excepting such as are pecuniary, for perpetuating Christianity at the Islands, are already there. Mr. Armstrong, the Minister of Instruction at the Islands, writing to one of the Secretaries of the American Board under date of January 2, 1856, bears this remarkable testimony :—

"During the year 1855, just closed," he says, "I visited all the Islands, and every missionary station, in the course of my official duty, and had good opportunities for seeing how the brethren conduct the affairs of their respective stations, and the success that has crowned their labors. I found them all at their posts, hard at work, watching for souls, and promoting the welfare of their people in various ways. As a class, they are very laborious and self-denying, and the advancement of their people in knowledge, industry, civilization and religion, is the best evidence of their success. I have lived for weeks on weeks among the natives, lodging with them in their huts, partaking of their homely fare and sleeping on their mats; and the more I see of them, the more I bless God for what he has done for them. I do not believe there is a community on earth, of the same number, more entirely pervaded by the blessed gospel. In the remotest corners of the land, I find a Bible and Hymn-book in nearly every house, if there was nothing else."

We may say of the faithful men, who, ceasing to be missionaries in the technical sense, are now laboring as pastors of churches, superintendents of education, or professors in the native College, or as physicians, teachers, editors, or Christian merchants:—"Except these abide in the ship, ye cannot be saved." Had the great body of these men left the Islands in the year 1848, the native government could not long have survived the catastrophe; and now, and for years to come, they will be, under God, the most effectual safeguard the Hawaiian Government and people can possibly have. Remaining there, with their numerous and healthy families of children, and furnished with facilities for educating those children, the government, the nation, the Islands will continue, with the ordinary blessing of Heaven, to be Christian, evangelical, a glorious monument of the triumphs of the gospel, a light enlightening the benighted groups lying far to the westward, and a cause for admiring gratitude to the whole Christian world!

Surely results like these are worth a great outlay for their preservation; but this cannot be effectually done without the speedy institution of a *College at the Islands*, where a portion of the children of foreign parents, and some of the more promising of the native youth, may receive that liberal education which is deemed so important in this country.

2. There is another and highly interesting view of the subject. This Christian community at the Sandwich Islands,—mixed in blood, but one in Christ,—should be regarded as a centre of light and influence for the large number of inhabited but benighted Islands scattered over the far and vast West of the Pacific Ocean. This missionary enterprise in the insular world beyond, besides its intrinsic importance, is among the necessary means, by its reacting influence, of raising the Hawaiian churches to the point of self-support and self-control; and its value, in this view, is already delightfully evident. The pecuniary means for supporting missionaries in Micronesia who are sent from the United States, must of course come in great measure from this country; but the support of missionaries and native assistants drawn from the Hawaiian churches, (as well as much of the labor connected with the details of the business,) may be thrown upon the 'Hawaiian Missionary Society,' which is independent of the American Board; and no small portion of the missionaries may at length be obtained from among the *alumni* of the *Oahu College*. Dr. Gulick, one of the first missionaries to Micronesia, is the son of a missionary at the Sandwich Islands, though educated in the United States; and the missionary children at the Islands are associated together to provide among themselves the means for his support. When the missionary ship, to be called the 'Morning-Star,' which has been requested for the mission in Micronesia, is actually in

those seas, the proposed institution for educating missionaries inured to the people and climate, will become a still more valuable auxiliary.

Thus we see, that the reasonable endowment of the Oahu College will be a good use of money for the upbuilding of Christ's kingdom at the Sandwich Islands, and for extending that kingdom through the islands of the great ocean beyond.

Funds and Buildings of the College.

The value of the property now belonging to the Oahu College, derived chiefly through the American Board, is estimated as follows:

Three hundred acres of land,	$9,000
College building, two stories,	7,000
Two dwelling houses,	6,000
Twelve lodging rooms,	2,000
Dining room, kitchen, etc.,	1,000
Out-houses,	500
Farming implements, herds, etc.,	1,500
Total,	$27,000

The land on which the buildings stand has an excellent and valuable spring of water, sufficient to irrigate it. There are one hundred acres in this lot, all enclosed by a good stone wall, and in part under cultivation. Another hundred acres adjoining, is also enclosed with a stone wall, and is devoted to pasturage. Another hundred acres of woodland lies about two miles distant. The buildings will suffice for the present.

An observer, familiar with the college edifices of the United States, may hardly be able to recognize a *College* in what he sees at Punahou. But what there is surpasses what were the ***visible beginnings*** of either Harvard, or Yale. Until the present time, moreover, there has been only a preparatory school. The first college class, and that a small one, commences the present year. A number of young men, once at Punahou, who would perhaps have been in the College had there been one, are at Williams, Yale, or some other of our American Colleges. Some have completed their preparations for life's business, and are preachers, missionaries, merchants, or connected with the government of the Islands.

The Endowment.

The cost of living at the Sandwich Islands has been materiallly increased by the settlement and mines of California. Just at present, it may not be easy to bring the expenses of a family at Punahou within the bounds recommended for the salaries of the officers of College. The arrangement for salaries should be based, however, on what we know to be the general course of things in the world. Fifteen hundred dollars, with the use of a house, is thought not to be too large a salary for the President of the Oahu College; and twelve hundred dollars, with the use of a house, for a Professor. The American Board will pay these two salaries for the years 1856 and 1857.

The Trustees propose to raise the sum of *fifty thousand dollars.* This is not too large a beginning. Of this sum the Hawaiian government engages to give ten thousand dollars, or one fifth part; on condition that the remaining forty thousand dollars be raised before July 6, 1858, and that the King have the right of nominating two of the twelve trustees of the College. The Prudential Committee have voted to subscribe five thousand dollars towards the endowment, on behalf of the American Board, payable in the year 1858.

It should be understood that, excepting the duty of approval or disapproval in respect to the election of members on the Board of Trustees, laid upon the American Board by the Charter for the space of twenty years, that

Board has no connection whatever with the College, or control of its proceedings. The College is an independent institution, sustaining no other relation to the Board, than it does to every other benefactor.

The Colleges of New England had generally some benevolent patron provided for them by Divine Providence;—a Harvard, a Yale, a Dartmouth, a Brown, a Bowdoin, a Williams; and the Colleges very properly took and embalmed their names in the memory of an enlightened and refined Christian community. These provided the general endowment. Many liberal men also founded particular professorships; or gave funds for the education of young men of talents and character, without the means of obtaining a liberal education. May the Lord raise up such benefactors for the Oahu College. That has grown, as the New England Colleges did, out of a great religious movement and the wonderful blessing of God on that movement. It has a religious object, and is controlled by a religious influence. The funds have every practicable guard from perversion. The permanent necessity for such an institution is apparent in the certainty of a permanent, rising, influential community on those admirably situated Islands. The independence of the Hawaiian Nation,—which, under present circumstances, is most favorable to its development,—is guaranteed by the United States, Great Britain and France; and the presumption of its falling under the dominion of a power foreign to us, is too small to deserve notice; and the influence of the College itself, as already described, will be one of the most effectual guards against such a result. There is not a finer climate in all the world. Were it true, that the native population is still wasting away, the effect of a corrupt commerce in old heathen times, still greater would be the need of such an institution. A flourishing community of some kind at the Sandwich Islands, there certainly will be; and the religious influences now at the Islands will be as available for that community, as hereafter developed, with whatever elements, as it will be for the one now existing.

A number of gentlemen have kindly consented, at the request of the Prudential Committee of the American Board of Commissioners for Foreign Missions, acting for the Trustees of the College, to take charge of the funds contributed in this country for the Oahu College, (where the donors do not direct them to be remitted directly to the Trustees at the Islands;) and they will invest such funds in the United States, and cause the interest to be remitted annually to the officer of the corporation legally authorized to receive it. The Trustees for the Fund, appointed in the first instance by the Prudential Committee, will fill the vacancies occurring in their own number; and they will be authorized to transfer the investment of the funds to the Sandwich Islands whenever they and the Trustees of the College concur in the opinion, that this can be safely and advantageously effected.

The following gentlemen compose the Trustees for the Funds to be invested in the United States; namely,—

Henry Hill, Esq., of Boston, Mass.
Pelatiah Perit, Esq., of New York city.
Gen. William Williams, of Norwich, Conn.
Hon. Thomas W. Williams, of New London, Conn.
Henry P. Haven, Esq., of New London, Conn.
James Hunnewell, Esq., of Charlestown, Mass.
William E. Dodge, Esq., of New York city.
Abner Kingman, Esq., of Boston, Mass.

Boston, August, 1856.

At a meeting of the Trustees of Oahu College, held at Honolulu, Oct. 27, 1856, the following resolutions were adopted with reference to the appointment of the Trustees for the Funds:

Resolved, 1. That the following gentlemen be and are hereby appointed Trustees, to receive, take charge of, and invest any funds that may have been, or hereafter may be contributed, in the United States, for the endowment of Oahu College; viz.,

Henry Hill, Esq., of Boston, Mass.
Pelatiah Perit, Esq., of New York city.
Gen. William Williams, of Norwich, Conn.
Hon. Thomas W. Williams, of New London, Conn.
Henry P. Haven, Esq., of New London, Conn.
James Hunnewell, Esq., of Charlestown, Mass.
William E. Dodge, Esq., of New York city.
Abner Kingman, Esq., of Boston, Mass.

Resolved, 2. That the Trustees appointed by the foregoing resolution be and are hereby authorized to fill all vacancies occurring in their own number; and that they be and are also further authorized to transfer the investment of any funds that may be received by them for the endowment of Oahu College, to the Sandwich Islands, whenever they and the Trustees of the said College concur in the opinion, that this can be safely and advantageously done.

The President of the College is now in this country to act for the Board of Trustees, under the following commission:

Honolulu, Sandwich Islands, Feb. 26, 1857.

Know all persons to whom these presents may come, that the Rev. Edward Griffin Beckwith, President of Oahu College, is duly appointed and authorized by the

Board of Trustees of this Institution to act as their agent in procuring funds, instructors, and books for the same; and to promote its general interests in all such ways as may be in his power, during his contemplated visit to the United States.

To this end, the Trustees of the College hereby bespeak for him the kind regards and co-operation of all the friends of education and religion with whom he may meet during his mission.

R. ARMSTRONG,
Sec'y of Board of Trustees.

At a meeting of the Trustees for the Fund, held in Boston, May 28, 1857, it was

Resolved, That the Rev. E. G. Beckwith, President of Oahu College, now in this country for the purpose of obtaining an endowment for that new and important Institution at the Sandwich Islands, be earnestly commended, by the Trustees for the Fund it is proposed to raise for the College in this country, to the liberal patronage of those who would promote the cause of education at the Islands, and thus give stability and perpetuity to the civil and Christian institutions which have been so successfully introduced into that part of the world; with the understanding, that the investment of the Fund be made under the direction of the aforesaid Trustees residing in the United States.

ABNER KINGMAN, *Clerk.*

The following is the form of subscription, which it is proposed to circulate among the friends of this enterprise:

We, the undersigned, subscribe the several sums set to our respective names, towards a Fund for the endowment of the Oahu College, in the Sandwich Islands, which

Fund is to be invested under the direction of a Board of Trustees in the United States appointed for this purpose by the Trustees of the College ; and the income arising therefrom to be annually appropriated to the support of said institution. Provided always, that no portion of said subscriptions, or any of the income arising therefrom, shall be used for the promotion of any system or course of education not in accordance with the Sixth Article of the present Charter of the said College.

Article Sixth of the Charter, reads as follows :

" Be it hereby further known, that, as the object of the Institution is the training of youth in the various branches of a Christian education, and, as it is reasonable that the Christian education should be in conformity to the general views of the founders and patrons of the Institution, no course of instruction shall be deemed lawful in said Institution, which is not accordant with the principles of Protestant Evangelical Christianity, as held by that body of Protestant Christians, in the United States of America, which originated the Christian Mission to these Islands; and to whose labors and benevolent contributions the people of these Islands are so greatly indebted."

Henry Hill, Esq., of Boston, Mass., Chairman of the Trustees for the Fund, is Treasurer of said Board of Trustees, and all remittances for the College can be made to him, at his office, 118 Milk St.

Boston, June 1, 1857.

www.ingramcontent.com/pod-product-compliance
Lightning Source LLC
LaVergne TN
LVHW020644110826
845149LV00004B/1353

* 9 7 8 1 4 1 8 1 9 0 8 4 2 *